Animal Parade

Charming Applique Quilts for Babies

DEDICATION

Contents

Nautical Whale Baby Quilt

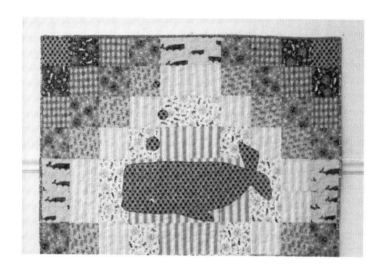

It's a very quick quilt to sew up! Here's a little mini tutorial for you:

Materials (for a 45" x 45" baby quilt):

1/4 yard of 9 fabrics

2 1/2 yards for backing

48" piece of batting

small scrap of black and white fabrics for the eye

lightweight fusible webbing

Whale Pattern

Begin by cutting out your 5" squares. You'll need to plan out where you'd like your fabrics and decide how many 5" squares of each fabric you'll need. Here's a layout guide for you:

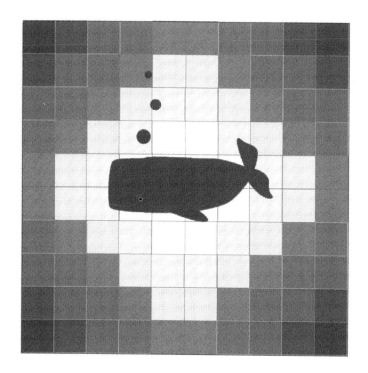

Sew your squares together in rows, then sew each row together.

Print out the whale pattern and tape it together. Cut out the whale shape, eye, and bubbles. Iron the fusible webbing to the back of the whale fabric and cut out the whale and bubbles. Iron the whale and bubbles to the quilt, using the above image as a placement guide.

Applique the whale and bubbles with a zig zag stitch.

Layer together the backing, batting and front and quilt as desired. I used a simplified bubble stitch. It was my first time and I think I can definitely use more practice, but it was fun to do!

Finish the quilt with binding and you're all ready to

show off your cute new whale quilt!

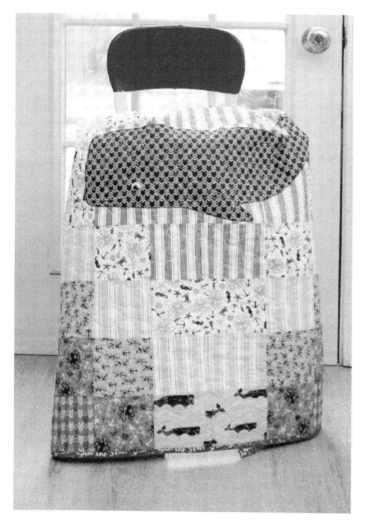

Whiskers: a Baby Quilt Pattern

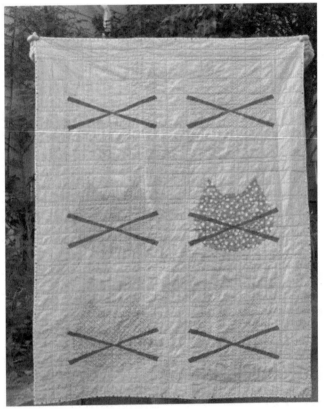

Fabric Requirements:

6 assorted quarter yards "cat face" fabrics (fat quarters work fine)

1/4 yard "whiskers" fabric

2 3/8 yards background fabric (or 2 1/2 yards if you're new to paper-piecing and want some extra wiggle room)

52"x67" batting

3 yds backing fabric or a pieced back of your choosing, measuring at least 53"x68"

3/8 yd binding fabric (for straight-cut 2 1/4" binding) **OR** 1/2 yd binding fabric (for straight-cut 2 1/2" binding)

Construction:

1. **Paper-piece** 6 "Whiskers" blocks as desired, and

square up to 15.5" (Block construction directions are included in the templates document). Fabric requirements will differ based on your method, but the recommendations above cover even the more wasteful techniques. If you're new to paper-piecing, check out this post for tutorials and resources, or this one on the way I like to paper-piece.

2. **Arrange** your cat blocks in three pairs.

3. **Sashing:** Trim selvages, and cut width of fabric (WOF) strips from background fabric for sashing as follows, using the diagram below if it helps:

(2) 5.25" strips

(1) 5" strip

(3) 5.5" strips

(2) 4.25" strips

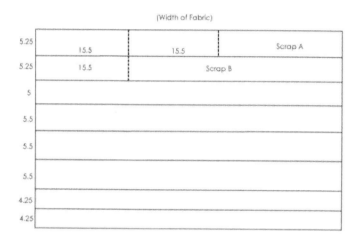

Refer to this diagram for steps 3-5

4. **Join <u>Pairs</u>:** From the first 5.25" strip, cut two 15.5" sections. We'll call the remaining fabric "Scrap A." From the second 5.25" strip, cut one 15.5"

section. We'll call the remaining fabric "Scrap B". Use the 5.25"x15.5" sections to join the three pairs of cat blocks to create three sets as pictured below.

5. **Join the three sets of pairs**: Trim "Scrap A" and "Scrap B" down to 5" wide, and join to the 5" WOF strip (end-to-end). From this looong piece of fabric, cut two 36" strips. Join to the three sets of pairs as pictured below, and trim any excess fabric.

6. **Attach side borders**: Join the three 5.5" strips, and cut two 56" strips for the vertical borders. Join to the

pieced center rectangle as pictured below. Trim any excess fabric.

7. **Attach top and bottom borders**: Measure the WOF of your two remaining 4.25" fabric strips. If you do not have enough length to cover the approximately 45" across the top and bottom of your quilt top, use scraps from steps 5 and 6 to extend the 4.25" strips to the required length. Attach to top and bottom as pictured below.

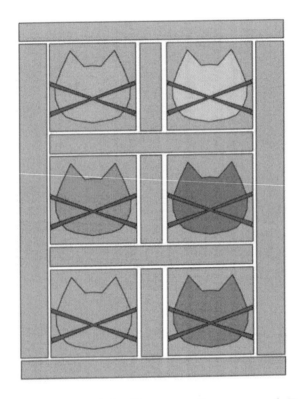

Refer to this diagram for steps 4-7

8. Trim quilt top and square up.

9. Assemble backing, batting, and quilt top. Quilt and bind as desired. Meow. Celebrate!

For my quilt, I used some spring green (and maybe

kiwi?) and aqua solids, along with leftover scraps from

the cat faces, to make a pieced backing.

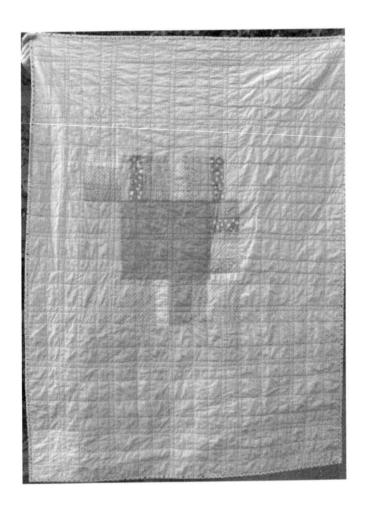

I quilted it in an irregular cross-hatch straight line pattern, and bound it with my favorite DS Quilts dots (I prefer 2 1/4-inch binding for a snug fit).

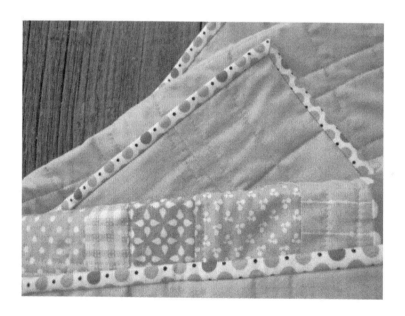

You could beef this pattern up to a larger size with additional cat blocks and/or wider sashing. Just one block would make a sweet pillow, I'd imagine.

I'm more often haphazardly "throwing some sashing

on," than following directions, so I'd welcome any feedback or questions about this pattern, especially if anything is confusing!

Fox Pattern

Materials

1.5 Yards White (background fabric)

2 Yards Fabric (back of quilt)

1/2 Yard Dark Color

1/2 Yard Medium Color

1/2 Yard Light Color

1/8 Yard Brown

1/4 Yard Dark Gray

1/4 Yard Light Gray

Batting (I like the fusible stuff myself)

6 yards Binding (wide double fold bias)

Thread for quilting

Freezer paper

Clear ruler

Rotary Cutter

Cut mat

Iron

Let's starts

To start, print and assemble the pattern, then trace all

the pattern pieces on to freezer paper. The black lines

are pattern lines, and the red lines mark all the sections (as well as pattern lines)

Each section will be sewn together in the order that it is numbered. Then the sections will all be sewn together to make the full fox. Once the fox (a rectangle) is assembled you will add borders around it to make it any size you want, I made a crib size for these (45"X60")

Cut out each pattern piece. Using a hot iron press the pattern piece on to the appropriate fabric. Then to cut them out, you are going to ad a 1/4" seam allowance along each edge. Using a clear ruler and rotary cutter line up the edge of the ruler along the pattern so the

1/4" is added to the edge. then trim.

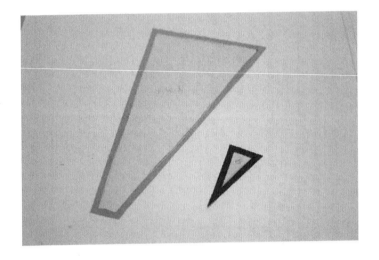

So each piece will look something like this, the pattern

piece with the edge all around.

*Tip, should you be making more than one like I did

here with the twin quilts, you can reuse the pattern

pieces, after the pieces are sewn together, peel the

pattern piece off and you can use it again by pressing it to fabric again.

With right sides together, sew two pieces together using the 1/4" seam allowance. Then press the seam allowance towards one side.

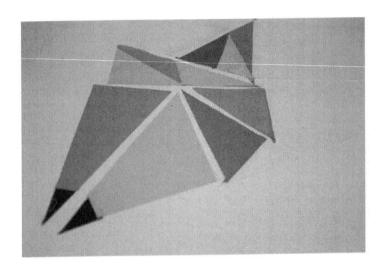

Here I have sections sewn together, next you will sew

the sections together.

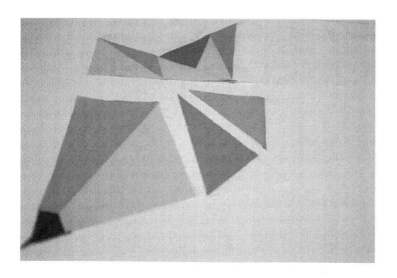

The sections aren't labeled in order, but you will sew them together in a similar order as you did the individual sections, small pieces together first, then larger sections together.

You will also sew half the fox together, and then the other half before sewing the whole fox together.

Once the fox is all sewn together, you can add details if you want, like eyes (I used scraps of felt) or a bow tie or hair bow.

Then add strips of fabric along the sides and top to make the quilt the desired size you want.

Then place the backing, batting, and top together and quilt the layers. I did a simple diamond quilting pattern.

Then trim up the edges as needed and sew on the binding.

Pull dogs and Panda

Materials

Fabric scraps

Scallop paper pieces (or download our free clamshell

template here

Thread and basic sewing kit

Animal appliqué templates (find these in our *Easy*

Curves book in issue 53)

How to cover and baste the scallop templates

Step 1

Take a paper scallop shape template and trim a piece of fabric to $\frac{1}{4}$in larger than than the template around every edge.

Step 2

Attach the paper template to the centre of a small piece of fabric and pin to hold in place. You can also use a binding clip for this too.

Step 3

With a knotted length of thread in your needle, take a large running stitch along the top curve within the seam allowance (*Fig 1*). Draw up the thread to gather

the fabric around the top of the template (*Fig 2*).

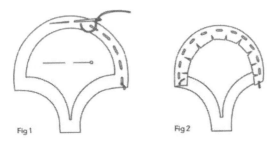

Fig 1   Fig 2

Step 4

Backstitch within the seam allowance to secure the

thread, and knot off.

Step 5

Press the curve well with a hot iron. Leave to cool

slightly, then remove the paper before pressing the

curve again.

Making the animal appliqué features

Step 6

Now it's time to have fun making the applique animal features. Trace the animal shape templates onto the paper side of fusible webbing and cut out. Fuse the shapes to the wrong side of your fabric, following the manufacturer's instructions, then cut out each shape neatly on the marked lines.

TIP: when cutting the appliqué features and ears, mark half of the pieces required and then turn your template over to mark out the remaining half – so that the pieces are cut as mirror images of each other.

Step 7

To make the ears, prepare the fabric shapes as above, then place two pieces right sides together (note if you're making the Owl design from issue 53, you fold each ear, instead of cutting multiples). Sew along the top of the ear – leaving the bottom open for turning. Clip V-shaped notches in the seam allowance at regular intervals, taking care to avoid cutting the stitching. Turn right side out and press. Repeat for the other ear.

Step 8

Now remove the backing paper from your animal's features and position the features onto one basted fabric scallop, referring to the animal pictures in our *Sewing Curves* book as a placement guide. Now fuse them in place and repeat for any remaining features.

Step 9

Use embroidery thread to add details such as eyes and mouths to your animals.

Attaching the ears

Step 10

Arrange all of your scallops onto a background fabric,

taking care to cover raw seam allowances with the basted curved pieces. Pin all of the scallops in place.

Step 11

To add the ears, tuck the raw fabric edges of the prepared shapes behind the scallop face using a seam allowance of $^3/8$in. Adjust the position as desired and pin into place.

Step 12

Appliqué the scallops in place, by hand or machine, stitching around the upper curve of each scallop. Once all of the scallops have been sewn in place, sew around each of the facial features to fully secure them.

Part 2: How to sew a bulldog mini quilt

You will need:

Background fabric $10\frac{1}{2}$in x 14in

Fabric to cover twenty-one (21) scallops + scraps for bulldog features

Fusible web for applique features

Embroidery thread for eyes

Batting 12in x 16in

Backing fabric 12in x 16in

Binding 21/2in x 70in

Twenty-one (21) 3½in scallop templates

Finished size

10in x 14in approx

Part 2: How to make a mini scalloped EPP

animals quilt

Step one

Follow steps 1–5 above to cover eighteen $3\frac{1}{2}$in scallops with print fabrics.

Step two

Make three Bulldog scallops, following steps 1–9 above.

Step three

Arrange your scallops over the background fabric, leaving approximately 3in at the top, and referring to the photo. Follow steps 10–12 to complete the quilt top.

Step four

Make a quilt sandwich with your batting and backing fabric. Quilt as desired. Trim away any excess batting and backing and bind the edges to complete.

Colorful Modern Heart Quilt

Let's starts:

First you'll need your supplies – I grabbed all of my

fabric at JoAnn cause it's close and easier than

ordering online when I get the idea that I want to do a

project that day   The backing is just an old sheet

that I had picked up at a garage sale – I love using

42

sheets in sewing projects!

I used the tutorial from Cluck Cluck Sew – it comes in different size heart options as well. I used the gray fabric instead of white for my background and really love it. I might look intimidating, but it's not! it's just some triangles sewed on to corners and then the heart sews each half together. The tutorial does a great job with step-by-step photos.

Next up I tried to get a feel for how I wanted the

squares to go – – this miss was not helping!!

The pattern just shows the hearts lining up under each other row after row, which is the easier way to go. I liked the look of the rows being staggered under one another when I laid it out:

So I ended up doing that. I cut some strips of gray to put in between the hearts and on the ends to space it out to where the rows where staggered. I sewed the hearts together to form a row and then sewed the rows together to start forming the quilt – it was so fun to see it start to take shape!!

After that I made the quilt sandwich and started

quilting through all the layers – I'm no pro!! I just

topstitched around each heart, starting with the

middle hearts and working my way out to the

edge hearts. Then I stitched some straight-line

quilting in between the hearts. All on my home

machine, which is totally doable!

You can see how fun the stitching is on the back with

the heart outlines:

48

I used some fun heart fabric for the binding, and planned it out so that when it was folded around the edge, you'd see half of the hearts on the front and their other halves on the back. I just love love love how it turned out!!

SO IF YOU'VE EVER WANTED TO TRY OUT

MAKING A COLORFUL MODERN HEART

QUILT, JUST GO FOR IT!!

Scrappy Star Quilt Tutorial

Materials:

- 10 fat quarters of Color Me Retro

- 1 1/2 yards of Pure Element solid in Lemonade

- 4 1/4 yards of backing fabric

- 2 1/4 yards of 90" wide batting

- 1/2 yard of binding fabric

- Coordinating thread

Finished Size: Approx 68" square

Seam Allowance: 1/4" unless otherwise noted

Cutting:

(WOF = Width of Fabric)

From each print

- Cut (1) 18"x18" square

From solid fabric:

- Cut (3) 18"xWOF strips

- Subcut each strip into (2) 18"x18" squares

Instructions:

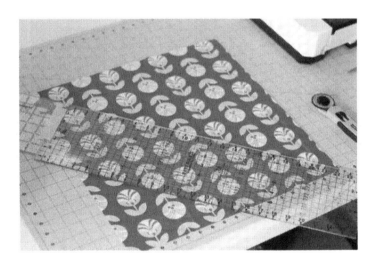

1. Cut each of the 18" squares and cut in half along

the diagonal. A 24" ruler isn't long

enough, you can extend it temporarily by taping

another ruler to one end. You should

have a total of 20 print triangles and 12 solid triangles.

2. Sew pairs of triangles together to create 16 blocks.

First pair up solid triangles with

print triangles, then pair up remaining print triangles.

Press seams open.

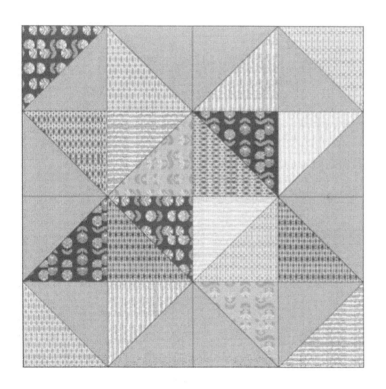

3. Arrange blocks using the diagram above. Sew

blocks together in each row. Press

seams in one direction, alternating every other row.

4. Sew rows together. Press seams open.

Baste, quilt, bind and enjoy!

Tiffany Diamonds Quilt

Materials:

Total of 48 ten inch squares (1 layer cake pack which has 42 squares + 3/4 yard of fabric cut into 6 squares)

Total of 96 five inch squares, same print (2 charm packs + 1 fat quarter cut into 6 squares)

65"x90" of backing fabric (about 4 yards)

Batting

Note: 1 yard of fabric = 12 ten inch or 48 five inch squares

Step 1: Sort all 48 of your ten inch squares into 12 piles of 4 squares each. As shown below, have each pile match with similar colors/prints.

Step 2: For each ten inch square (all 48), do the following Steps A-E:

A) Take 2 five inch squares, and on each square mark a diagonal line from corner to corner. As shown below, I used a Hera marker which is a plastic tool that creates a crease on the fabric when pressed with a firm hand. With a Hera marker, you can layer the fabric (~2 layers), and the crease will show through both layers.

If you don't have a Hera marker, simply draw a line using a ruler and pen, or fold the square diagonal and press with an iron and then unfold.

B) Align 1 five inch square along the top left corner of a ten inch square. Make sure the placement of the diagonal line is the same as below.

61

Pin in place, and then sew directly along the diagonal

line:

C) As shown below, cut a ¼" seam along the left outer part of the diagonal line that so that the corner comes off.

Up-close photo (be sure to cut a 1/4" allowance from the stitched line):

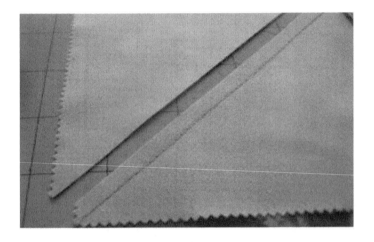

D) Press open with an iron:

E) Repeat steps B through D, but on the bottom

right corner of the ten inch square.

Step 3: After completing Step 2 for all 48 ten inch squares, you can assemble the piles of 4 that you sorted in Step 1. First, arrange the 4 blocks as shown below. Sew the top 2 blocks together and then the bottom 2 blocks together to create 2 units.

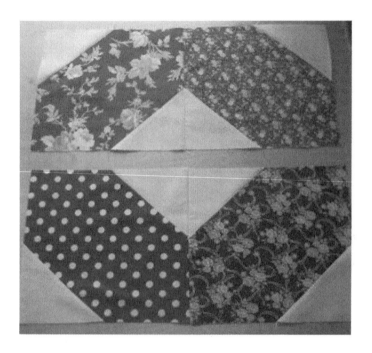

Last, sew the top and bottom units together.

(**Note for Newbies:** when I refer to sewing, sew with the right sides facing together, sew a ¼" seam, and then press open with an iron). **Step 4:** Arrange your finished blocks in 4 rows of 3 blocks each.

Start by sewing each of the 3 blocks in each row together. And then sew each row together to create the pieced quilt top.

Step 5: Baste and quilt it! For this one, I decided to tie it (shown below) rather than machine quilt. Click the following for a tutorial on How to Tie a Quilt. If you've never done it before, you'll love it because it's quick and you don't have to worry about the fabric layers puckering like you do when machine quilting. It

looks great too, and makes for a much fluffier quilt.

Step 6: Bind it

>Tip!: Save the corners you cut from Step 2c. You can use them for an easy half square triangle scrap quilt project down the ro

Made in the USA
Middletown, DE
20 February 2022